# Beliefs Without Borders

## Pathway To A New Future™ *Book I*

*By Carlino Giampolo*

# Beliefs Without Borders
## Pathway To A New Future™ *Book I*

Translated into Arabic by Adly Mirza.

ترجمه إلى العربيه عدلي ميرزا.

Translated into Chinese by Suzanne Zeng.

中文译者：鄭舒。

Translated into French by Sarah Pouzet.

Traduit en français par Sarah Pouzet.

Translated into German by Stephanie Rózsa.

Übersetzt ins Deutsche von Stephanie Rózsa.

Translated into Hebrew by Amir Yoeli.

תרגום לעברית ע"י אמיר יואלי.

Translated into Italian by Giuliano Sorelo.

Traduzione in italiano di Giuliano Sorelo.

Translated into Japanese by Kakuko Shoji.

日本語訳 庄司香久子。

Translated into Russian by Alexander Vovin.

Перевел на русский Александр Вовин.

Translated into Spanish by José Gigante.

Traducido al Español por José Gigante.

ISBN: 0-937827-03-7

My deepest gratitude to each translator and to
Dr. James Cascaito and Mr. James Winpenny for their
editorial assistance. Special thanks to all my teachers,
especially at the metaphysical organizations,
Silva Mind Control and Concept Synergy.

Typography, back cover design and print production by
Blaine Fergerstrom, ZZ Type, Honolulu, Hawaii

Published by Carlino & Company
P.O. Box 15182, Honolulu, Hawaii 96830
(808) 926-1752

You may purchase additional copies of this book at:

**www.BeliefsWithoutBorders.com**

Visit our other Web Sites at:
www.TheArtOfLettingGo.com
www.GolfMagic.us
www.TheLandOfAloha.com
www.Carlino.us

The book's intent is to assist in creating a
new world of greater love and peace.

الغرض من هذا الكتاب، المساعدة فى خلق عالم
جديد يشمله حب عظيم و أمان.

此书的目的是帮助创造一个充满更多爱与和平的新
世界。

L'intention de ce livre est d'aider à la création d'un
monde nouveau, avec plus d'amour et de paix.

Ziel dieses Buches ist es, dazu beizutragen, eine
neue Welt herbeizuführen, in der mehr Liebe und
Frieden herrscht.

כוונת הספר לעזור ביצרת עולם חדש עם יותר אהבה ושלום.

L'intento di questo libro è di contribuire alla
creazione di un mondo nuovo pervaso di più amore
e pace.

この本は、大いなる愛と平和に恵まれた新しい世界を築く
ために役立てたいという意図で書かれたものです。

Задача книги  помочь в создании нового
общества, в котором будет больше любви
и мира.

La intención de este libro es de ayudar a crear un
nuevo mundo de más amor y paz.

Beliefs are the foundation upon which you build your future.

إن الايمان هو الأساس الذى يبنى عليه مستقبلك.

信念是建造将来的基础。

Les croyances sont la fondation sur laquelle chacun construit son avenir.

Glaube ist die Basis, auf der du deine Zukunft aufbaust.

אמונות הן הבסיס עליו נבנה עתידך.

Ciò in cui credi costituisce il fondamento su cui costruisci il tuo futuro.

信念は己れの将来を基く為の礎である。

Вера – фундамент, на котором ты строишь своё будущее.

Las creencias son los cimientos sobre los cuales construyes tu futuro.

The power of a belief is derived from the
attention you give to it.

قوة الايمان تنبثق من مدى إهتمامك بعقيدة
الايمان.

信念的力量来源于对信念的关注。

La force d'une croyance provient de l'intérêt qu'on
lui porte.

Die Kraft des Glaubens ist so stark wie die
Aufmerksamkeit, die du ihm gibst.

כוח האמונה נובע מתשומת הלב הניתנת לה.

Il potere di un convincimento discende
dall'attenzione che gli presti.

信念の強さはそれを信じることから生まれでるものである。

Могущество веры происходит от внимания,
которое ты ей посвящаешь.

El poder de una creencia proviene de la atención
que le das.

Belief precedes experience.

العقيدة تسبق الايمان.

信念胜于经验。

La croyance précède l'expérience.

Der Glaube geht der Erfahrung voraus.

האמונה קודמת לנסיון.

Il credere precede l'esperienza.

信念なくして経験はあり得ない。

Вера предшествует опыту.

La creencia precede la experiencia.

Change your beliefs and your experiences
will change.

إذا تغير إيمانك تغيرت تجاربك.

信念改变，体验也会随着改变。

Changez vos croyances et vos expériences
changeront.

Ändere deinen Glauben, und deine Erfahrungen
werden sich ändern.

שנה את אמונותיך וישתנו חוויותיך.

Cambia i tuoi convincimenti, e cambieranno le tue
esperienze.

信念が変われば体験する事柄も自ずから変わってくる。

Измени веру и твой жизненный опыт
изменится.

Cambia tus creencias y cambiarás tus experiencias.

Inherent goodness is the essence of being human.

الطيبة الباطنية هي من طابع البشر.

人的本质在于天性的良善。

La bonté innée est l'essence d'être humain.

Ein gutes Wesen ist das, was den Menschen ausmacht.

טוב לב הינו תמצית היותך אנושי.

L'innata bontà è l'essenza dell'essere umano.

天性の美徳こそ人間であることの本質である。

Врожденная добродетель есть сущность человека.

La bondad inherente es la esencia de ser humano.

Respect every person's inherent goodness.

إحترم الطيبه الباطنيه لكل أنسان.

尊重每个人与天俱来的良善。

Respecte la bonté innée de chacun.

Respektiere das Gute in jedem.

כבד את טוב לבו של כל אדם.

Rispetta l'innata bontà di ogni individuo.

個々のもつ善性を尊重しなさい。

Почитай врожденную добродетель каждого человека.

Respeta la bondad inherente de cada persona.

Every person's life has value and
significance.

حياة كل شخص لها قيمة وفعالية.

每个生命都有其价值与意义。

La vie de chaque individu a de la valeur et du sens.

Das Leben eines jeden Menschen ist wertvoll und
bedeutend.

חייו של כל אדם הינם בעלי ערך ומשמעות.

La vita di ogni individuo possiede valore e senso.

人それぞれの命に価値があり意義がある。

Жизнь каждого человека имеет ценность и
смысл.

La vida de cada persona tiene valor y significado.

Human dignity is too precious to permit the
taking of another's life.

الكرامة الإنسانية لاتسمح بايجاز سلب حياة إنسان
آخر .

人的生命如此宝贵，不容夺走。

La dignité humaine est trop précieuse pour
permettre que l'on ôte la vie d'autrui.

Die Würde des Menschen ist zu wertvoll, als dass
das Töten eines anderen je gebilligt werden dürfte.

ערך האדם יקר מדי מלאפשר גזלת חיי אחר.

La dignità umana è troppo preziosa per permettere
che si prenda la vita altrui.

他の命の略奪を許容するには 人間の尊厳はあまり
にも貴重である。

Человеческое достоинство слишком
драгоценно, чтобы позволить отнять жизнь
другого человека.

La dignidad humana es muy preciosa para permitir
quitarle la vida a otro.

Less violence in your own life will result in
less violence in the world.

الإ قلال من العنف فى حياتك يأتى  بالتالى على
إقلال العنف في العالم.

减少个人暴力会减少世界暴力。

Moins de violence dans votre vie entraînera une
diminution de la violence dans le monde.

Weniger Gewalt in deinem eigenen Leben wird zu
weniger Gewalt in der Welt führen.

פחות אלימות בחייך תישא פחות אלימות בעולם.

Meno violenza nella tua vita personale determinerà
meno violenza nel mondo.

個々の生活の中の暴力をなくしていけば、世の中の暴力も
消滅 していくであろう。

Чем меньше насилия в твоей собственной
жизни, тем меньше насилия в мире.

Menos violencia en tu propia vida resultará en
menos violencia en el mundo.

Express the depth of your emotions without harming anyone.

عبر عن أعماق عواطفك دون أن تمس بالآخرين.

用无伤的方式表达强烈的情感。

Exprimez la profondeur de vos émotions sans blesser autrui.

Zeige deine tiefsten Gefühle, ohne andere damit zu verletzen.

בטא את עומק רגשותיך מבלי לפגוע באחר.

Esprimi la profondità delle tue emozioni senza ledere nessuno.

自分の深層にある感情は誰も傷つけないように心して表わすべきである。

Выражая глубину своих чувств, не наноси вреда другим.

Expresa la profundidad de tus emociones sin hacerle daño a nadie.

Be responsible for your actions and the
effects of your actions.

كن مسؤولاً عن أعمالك و نتائج تاثيرها.

对自己的行为负责，对行为的后果负责。

Assumez la responsabilité et les conséquences de
vos actes.

Übernehme Verantwortung für dein Handeln und
seine Folgen.

היה אחראי למעשיך ולתוצאות הנלוות להן.

Assumi la responsabilità delle tue azioni e delle
conseguenze delle tue azioni.

己れの行動とその結果に責任をもちなさい。

Будь ответственным за свои действия и их
последствия.

Sé responsable de tus actos y de los efectos de tus
actos.

You are accountable for every choice you
make in life.

إختياراتك في الحياة ناتجة عن مسئوليتك لها.

要对生活中所作的决定负责。

Vous êtes responsable de chaque décision que vous
prenez dans la vie.

Du selbst bist verantwortlich für jede Entscheidung,
die du im Leben triffst.

הינך אחראי לכל שתבחר בחייך.

Sei responsabile di ogni scelta che fai nella vita.

人生において自分が選択したことには自分自身が責任をと
るべきである。

Ты ответственен за каждый выбор в своей
жизни.

Eres responsable de cada elección que haces en
la vida.

It's is better to be understanding than to be understood.

فهمك للآخرين أفضل من فهم الآخرين لك.

要求他人的理解，不如先理解他人。

Mieux vaut être compréhensif que compris.

Verständnis für andere ist wichtiger als verstanden zu werden.

טוב להבין מאשר להיות מובן.

È meglio comprendere che essere compresi.

他人に理解される立場より理解する立場におかれた方がいい。

Важнее понимать, чем быть понятым.

Es mejor comprender que ser comprendido.

Respect every person's spirituality.

إحترم ديانة الآخرين.

尊重他人的信仰。

Respectez la spiritualité de chaque individu.

Respektiere die Spiritualität eines jeden.

כבד את רוחניותו של כל אדם.

Rispetta la spiritualità di ogni individuo.

人それぞれの精神を尊重しなさい。

Уважай духовность каждого человека.

Respeta la espiritualidad de cada persona.

Every human being is unique.

يختلف كل إنسان عن الآخر.

每个人都独一无二。

Chaque être humain est unique.

Jeder Mensch ist einzigartig.

כל אדם מיוחד הוא.

Ciascun essere umano è unico.

十人十色、皆それなりにユニークなのだ。

Каждый человек уникален.

Cada ser humano es único.

In the truest sense, every human being is
neither superior nor inferior to another.

فى المعنى الحقيقى، لايكون الانسان أعلى أو
أقل شأنًا من غيره.

其实，我们不比他人高贵，也不比他人低贱。

Au sens le plus pur, chaque être humain n'est ni
supérieur, ni inférieur aux autres.

Tatsächlich ist kein Mensch einem anderen über-
oder unterlegen.

לאמיתו של דבר, כל אדם אינו עליון או נחות מאחר.

Nel senso più  autentico, ogni essere umano non è
né superiore né inferiore a un altro.

真の意味において見れば人はみな同等、上もなく下もない。

Воистину каждый человек не лучше и не
хуже других.

En el sentido más cierto, ningún ser humano es
mejor ni peor que otro.

Making judgments often leads to pain for
oneself and for others.

حكمك للآخرين يؤدى بالألم لك وللآخرين.

论断常会为自己与他人带来痛苦。

Juger les autres mène souvent à la souffrance pour
soi-même et pour autrui.

Wenn du urteilst, fügst du dir und anderen oft
Schaden zu.

ביקורתיות לעתים מביאה לכאב עצמי ולזולת.

Esprimere giudizi spesso conduce alla sofferenza
propria e altrui.

人を批判することは、自分にとっても他の人たちにとっても
苦痛の種となることが多い。

Осуждение часто приносит страдание себе и
другим.

Juzgar a menudo le causa dolor a uno mismo y a
otros.

Do not label a person and then judge the
label.

لاتصف الآخرين و تحكم على ما وصفته.

别将人规类，又对那类别有偏见。

Ne cataloguez pas une personne pour ensuite la
juger.

Stemple niemanden ab um dann über ihn zu
urteilen.

אין לסווג אדם ולהעביר ביקורת על הסווג.

Non etichettare una persona per poi giudicarne
l'etichetta.

人を先入観で評価し判断してはいけない。

Не наклеивай ярлык человеку и не суди
потом по этому ярлыку.

No etiquetes a una persona y luego juzgues la
etiqueta.

Hatred keeps us tied to the past.

الحقد ببقيدنا بماضينا.

仇恨令我们与过去纠缠。

La haine nous maintient attachés au passé.

Hass fesselt uns an die Vergangenheit.

שנאה קושרת אותנו אל העבר.

L'odio ci tiene legati al passato.

憎しみは我々を過去に縛り付ける。

Ненависть привязывает нас к прошлому.

El odio nos mantiene atados al pasado.

The ability to act without harming anyone is
the basis of real power.

أساس القوة الحقيقية هى القدرة على العمل
دون الأضرار بالآخرين.

真正的权力建立在无伤的行为之上。

La capacité d'agir sans blesser autrui est la base du
vrai pouvoir.

Die Fähigkeit zu Handeln ohne jemandem Schaden
zuzufügen ist die Basis wahrer Kraft.

היכולת מבלי לפגוע בזולת הינה בסיס לעוצמה אמיתית.

La capacità di agire senza danneggiare nessuno
costituisce la base del vero potere.

他の人々を傷つけることなく行動できる力こそ真の力の礎と
なるものである。

Возможность действовать, не нанося вреда
кому бы то ни было, есть настоящее
могущество.

La abilidad de actuar sin hacerle daño a nadie es la
base del verdadero poder.

Forgive yourself first and then forgive others.

أعفو عن نفسك أولاً ثم أعفي عن الآخرين.

宽恕自己，再宽恕他人。

Pardonnez-vous d'abord puis pardonnez aux autres.

Vergib zuerst dir selbst und dann anderen.

סלח לעצמך ואז תסלח לאחרים.

Perdona a te stesso prima di perdonare agli altri.

人を許す前にまず自分を許しなさい。

Прощай себя, чтобы прощать других.

Perdónate primero a ti mismo y luego perdona a
los demás.

Forgive others either for what they have
done, or for why they have done it.

أعفو عن الآخرين بما فعلوا أو لماذا فعلوا.

若不能宽恕他人的行为，至少宽恕他们的动机。

Pardonnez aux autres soit pour ce qu'ils ont fait,
soit pour la raison qui les ont poussés à le faire.

Vergib anderen was sie getan haben und weshalb sie
es getan haben.

סלח לאחרים על שעשו או על הסיבה שבגינה עשו מה שעשו.

Perdona agli altri sia per ciò che hanno fatto che per
le ragioni per cui l'hanno fatto.

何をしたか何故したかにかかわらず、その人達を許しなさい。

Прощай других за то, что они совершили
или за то, почему они это совершили.

Perdona a los demás por lo que han hecho, o por las
razones que tuvieron para hacerlo.

Attempting to be perfect leads to pain.

قد تؤدي محاولة التكامل إلى الألم.

追求完美会带来痛苦。

Essayer d'être parfait mène à la souffrance.

Das Streben nach Perfektion verursacht Schmerz.

נסיון להיות מושלם מביא לכאב.

Mirare alla perfezione porta al dolore.

完璧であろうとするとやがて傷つくことになる。

Попытка быть совершенным ведет к страданию.

Tratar de ser perfecto causa dolor.

Choose excellence rather than perfection.

أختار الامتياز عن التكامل.

但求卓越，不求完美。

Choisissez l'excellence plutôt que la perfection.

Sei lieber hervorragend als perfekt.

בחר בהצטיינות על פני שלמות.

Scegli l'eccellenza piuttosto che la perfezione.

完璧であることより卓越していることを目指しなさい。

Предпочти высокие качества совершенству.

Elige la excelencia en lugar de la perfección.

Sharing of oneself is the very foundation
of love.

أساس الحب هو فعالية مساهمة الذات.

奉献自己是爱的根基。

Le partage de soi est la fondation même de l'amour.

Von sich selbst zu geben ist das Fundament der
Liebe.

היכולת לחלוק את עצמך הינה היסוד לאהבה.

Donarsi agli altri è l'autentico fondamento
dell'amore.

分かち合うことなくして愛は存在し得ない。

Отдача себя –основание любви.

Entregarse uno mismo es la base misma del amor.

To create something of value, you have to
give of yourself.

لأجل إبتكار شئ ما ذو قيمة، عليك التفاني فيه.

要创造价值，必须贡献自己。

Pour créer quelque chose de valeur, vous devez
donner de vous-même.

Um etwas Wertvolles zu vollbringen, musst du dich
der Sache hingeben.

על מנת ליצור דבר בעל ערך, עליך לתת מעצמך.

Per creare qualcosa che abbia valore, bisogna che tu
dia te stesso.

価値あるものを創る為には身を捨ててかかるべきである。

Чтобы создать что-либо ценное, ты должен
отдать частицу себя.

Para crear algo que valga, tienes que dar de
ti mismo.

When you give freely of yourself you are
always the recipient.

السخاء يعود بالفائد إليك.

无私地奉献，必有收获。

Lorsque vous donnez de vous-même librement,
vous êtes toujours le bénéficiaire.

Wenn du großzügig gibst, bist du immer der
Beschenkte.

כאשר אתה נותן מעצמך בנדיבות, אתה תמיד זוכה.

Quando dai te stesso, ne ricavi sempre benefici.

善行は必ず自分に戻ってくるもの。

Когда ты свободно отдаешь себя, ты всегда
приобретаешь.

Cuando das de ti mismo libremente serás también
el recipiente.

Giving of yourself, simply for the joy of giving, is the highest form of giving.

عطاء النفس في سبيل العطاء هو من أسمى العطاءات.

因喜乐而奉献自己是奉献的最高境界。

Donnez de vous-même, pour le simple plaisir de donner, est le don ultime.

Von sich selbst zu geben, nur um des Gebens willen, ist die höchste Form des Gebens.

לתת מעצמך, אך ורק בשביל לתת, זהו הערך העליון של נתינה.

Dare se stessi semplicemente per la gioia di dare costituisce la forma più alta del dono.

最高の寄与の形、それは 報酬を求めることなく只ひたすら他に尽くすことである。

Отдача себя просто из радости отдавать есть высочайшая форма отдачи.

Dar de ti mismo, por el simple hecho de dar, es la más noble forma de dar.

Make choices which offer you the greatest
freedom without harming anyone.

إجعل إختياراتك وافره  لأقصى معاني الحرية
دون الإضرار بالآخرين.

做出带来自由又不伤害他人的选择。

Prenez des décisions qui vous offrent la plus grande
liberté sans porter atteinte à autrui.

Triff Entscheidungen die dir die größtmöglichen
Freiheiten lassen ohne jemandem damit zu schaden.

בחר באשר יביא לך את מירב החופש ולא יפגע באחרים.

Fai scelte che ti offrano la maggiore libertà senza
nuocere a nessuno.

誰も傷つけることなく最大の自由が与えられる、そんな選択
をしなさい。

Совершай выбор, предлагающий тебе
величайшую свободу, не причиняя вреда
никому.

Elige lo que te dé más libertad sin hacerle daño
a nadie.

Be willing to accept that you may be wrong at times, in your pursuit of what is right.

عند سعيك للحقيقة عليك قبول أخطائك في بعض الأحيان.

追求真理的同时要接受自己犯错的可能。

Dans votre poursuite de la vérité, soyez prêt à accepter que vous puissiez parfois avoir tort.

Akzeptiere bereitwillig, dass du zeitweise unrecht hast auf deiner Suche nach dem Richtigen.

היה מוכן לקבל טעויותיך לפרקים בחיפוש הצדק.

Accetta di buon grado di poter essere a volte in errore nella ricerca di ciò che è giusto.

何が正しいかを追求するならば、自分も時には過ちを犯すかもしれないのだということを素直に認めなさい。

Будь готов признать, что ты можешь быть иногда неправ в твоих поисках правды.

Está dispuesto a aceptar que te puedes equivocar a veces, en tu búsqueda de lo correcto.

When you fail at times you are not a failure.

إذا فشلت أحياناً لاتعتبر نفسك فشلاً.

偶尔失败并不等于你是失败者。

Lorsque parfois vous échouez, vous n'êtes pas perdant.

Ab und zu Fehler zu machen heißt nicht, ein Versager zu sein.

באם תכשל, אינך כשלון.

Seppure a volte fallisci, non per questo sei un fallimento.

失敗したからといって、それで敗者となるわけではない。

Когда ты терпишь иногда неудачу, это не крах.

Cuando fallas a veces no eres un fracaso.

To achieve greatness, explore what you do
not know.

لتنجز شئ عظيم عليك إستكشاف مالا تعرفه.

探索未知是通向成就的途径。

Pour atteindre la grandeur, explorez ce que vous ne
connaissez pas.

Um Größe zu erlangen, lerne Dinge die du noch
nicht weißt.

בכדי להגיע לגדולה, עליך לחקור את שאינך יודע.

Per pervenire alla grandezza, esplora ciò che non
conosci.

偉大なる目標を達成するためには、まず自分の見知らぬ
物事を探究することから始めなさい。

Чтобы достичь величия, изучи то,что ты не
знаешь.

Para alcanzar la grandeza, explora lo que
desconoces.

Learn and grow from the joyful and
sorrowful experiences in your life.

تعلم و أنمو من تجارب أفراحك و أحزانك.

在喜怒哀乐的体验中学习、成长。

Apprenez et enrichissez-vous à travers vos
expériences joyeuses et douloureuses.

Lerne und wachse an den schönen und traurigen
Erfahrungen in deinem Leben.

למד והתפתח מהניסיונות השמחים והעגומים בחייך.

Apprendi e matura attraverso le esperienze liete e
dolorose della vita.

人生の悲喜こもごもの経験から学びそして成長しなさい。

Учись и мужай благодаря радостным и
скорбным опытам твоей жизни.

Crece y aprende de las experiencias alegres y tristes
en tu vida.

Identify and take away who you are not, and you will discover more of who you are.

تعرف بما لا أنت فيه حتى تكون أكثر معرفة بنفسك.

剔除与自己不相合的，就能发觉真正的自我。

Identifiez et supprimez ce que vous n'êtes pas, vous découvrirez ainsi davantage qui vous êtes.

Entdecke wer du nicht bist und du wirst mehr zu dem wer du wirklich bist.

זהה וסלק את מי שאינך ותגלה יותר מעצמך.

Individua e sbarazzati di ciò che non sei, e avrai maggiori possibilità di scoprire chi sei.

偽りの己れを取り去った時、真の自分を見い出すだろう。

Познай себя и отбрось, что не есть ты, и ты откроешь больше о своей сущности.

Identifica y deshazte de quien no eres, y descubrirás más sobre quien eres.

Ideals and principles have to be put into
action for them to have value.

المبادئ والمثالية عليها أن تطبق لإبراز فائدتها.

没有实践的理想和原则不过是一纸空文。

Les idéaux et les principes doivent être mis en
oeuvre pour avoir de la valeur.

Ideale und Vorsätze müssen in die Tat umgesetzt
werden um an Wert zu gewinnen.

יש ליישם רעיונות ועקרונות בכדי שיהה להם ערך.

Ideali e principi richiedono d'essere messi in atto
per essere validi.

理想と主義は、行動にうつされて始めて価値あるものと
なる。

Идеалы и принципы должны быть введены в
действие, чтобы иметь ценность.

Los ideales y principios deben ponerse en acción
para que tengan valor.

The method you choose for achieving a goal
reveals your character.

أسلوبك المختار للوصول إلى هدف يبرز حقيقة
شخصيتك.

一个人达到目标的方式显出他的品格。

La méthode que vous choisissez pour atteindre un
objectif révèle votre caractère.

Die Methoden die du wählst, um deine Ziele zu
erreichen, enthüllen deinen Charakter.

דרך הפעולה להשגת פעולה משקפת את אופיך.

Il metodo che scegli per realizzare un obiettivo
rivela il tuo carattere.

目標を達成するためにどのような術（すべ）が選ばれるかを
見れば、その人の人格が分かる。

Метод, который ты выбираешь для
достижения цели, обнаруживает твой
характер.

El método que eliges para realizar tus metas revela
tu carácter.

Life is a mystery.

الحياة كلها غموض.

人生是一个迷。

La vie est un mystère.

Das Leben ist ein Mysterium.

החיים תעלומה.

La vita è mistero.

人生とは不可解なものである。

Жизнь есть таинство.

La vida es un misterio.

Spirituality blossoms continuously and can never be fully understood.

تنمو الروحانية بإستمرار ويصعب فهمها.

灵性不断发展，但永不被完全了解。

La spiritualité s'épanouit continuellement et ne peut jamais être totalement comprise.

Spiritualität wächst ständig, sie kann nie völlig verstanden werden.

רוחניות פורחת ברציפות ולעולם לא תובן במלואה.

La spiritualità sboccia di continuo e non può mai essere del tutto compresa.

精神は常に開花し続けるが、理解し尽くすことは不可能である。

Духовность цветет непрерывно и никогда не может быть полностью понята.

La espiritualidad florece continuamente y nunca es completamente entendida.

Everything possesses spirituality.

كل شئ يمتلك روحانيته.

天下众物皆有灵性。

Chaque chose possède une spiritualité.

Alles besitzt Spiritualität.

בכל דבר קיימת רוחניות.

Tutto possiede spiritualità.

森羅万象、魂の宿らぬものはない。

Всё обладает духовностью.

Todo posee espiritualidad.

Divine love does not have to be earned and can never be lost.

ليس من الواحب كسب الحب الالهى كما أنه لا يفقد أبدًا.

圣爱无偿，且不会遗失。

L'amour divin n'a pas besoin d'être mérité et ne peut jamais être perdu.

Göttliche Liebe kann man sich nicht verdienen aber auch nicht verlieren.

אין לזכות באהבה אלוהית ואין לאבדה.

Non si può mai conquistare l'amore divino né mai perderlo.

神聖な愛とは、努めずしてかち得る愛であり、永遠に消滅することのない愛である。

Божественная любовь не должна быть заслужена и не может быть утрачена.

El amor divino no necesita ser ganado y tampoco puede ser perdido.

Be the creator of your own destiny.

كن المدبر لمصيرك.

创造自己的命运。

Soyez le créateur de votre propre destinée.

Sei deines eigenen Schicksals Schmied.

היה היוצר של גורלך.

Sii l'artefice del tuo proprio destino.

己の運命の創造者となりなさい。

Будь творцом своей собственной судьбы.

Sé el creador de tu propio destino.

True destiny is self-chosen.

مصيرك الحقيقي اختيار ذاتك.

我命在我不在天。

Chacun choisit sa destinée véritable.

Das wahre Schicksal ist selbst gewählt.

גורל אמיתי הינו תוצר של בחירה עצמית.

Il vero destino si sceglie da sé.

真の運命は自分で選ぶもの、他人に与えられるものではない。

Истинная судьба избирается тобой.

El verdadero destino lo eliges tú mismo.

Hope for the future is the motivator for change and growth.

أمل المستقبل هو الحافز للتغير والنمو.

对将来的期望是改过与成长的动机。

L'espoir dans l'avenir stimule le changement et la croissance.

Die Hoffnung auf die Zukunft ist Antrieb für Veränderung und Wachstum.

תקווה לעתיד הינה המוליך לשינוי וגדילה.

La speranza nel futuro sprona a cambiare e maturare.

将来への希望が人の生き方を変え、成長を促す。

Надежда на будущее – движущий фактор для изменений и роста.

La esperanza en el futuro es la motivación para el cambio y el crecimiento.

Where you are going is more valuable to
you than where you have been.

أين ستصل أكثر تمنًا مما كنت فيه سابقًا.

未来的走向比过去的旅程更重要。

Le lieux vers lequel vous allez à plus de valeur à
vos yeux que les endroits d'où vous venez.

Wohin du gehst ist wichtiger als woher du kommst.

המקום שאליו פניך מועדות הינו בעל ערך רב יותר
מאשר המקום בו היית.

Il luogo verso cui procedi ha maggior valore di
quello in cui sei stato.

より大切なのは、その人が 過去においてどうあったかでは
なくこれからどうなるかということである 。

Куда ты идешь – ценнее для тебя, чем где ты
был.

Hacia donde vas es más valioso que donde
has estado.

Your future depends upon the attitude with which you approach it.

يعتمد مستقبلك على التحكم في تصرفاتك.

一个人的将来取决于他面对将来的态度。

Votre avenir dépend de l'attitude avec laquelle vous l'approchez.

Deine Zukunft hängt davon ab, wie du ihr entgegen trittst.

עתידך מוטל בגישתך כלפיו.

Il tuo futuro dipende dall'atteggiamento con cui lo affronti.

人の将来は、その人がどのように生きていくかによって定まる。

Твое будущее зависит от точки зрения, с которой ты приближаешься к нему.

Tu futuro depende de la actitud con la que lo enfoques.

The future always offers us the opportunity
to become happier.

يمنح المستقبل دائمًا فرص السعادة.

未来提供更幸福的机遇。

L'avenir nous offre toujours l'opportunité d'être
plus heureux.

Die Zukunft bietet uns immer die Möglichkeit,
glücklicher zu werden.

העתידתמיד מביא הזדמנויות להיות שמח יותר.

Il futuro offre sempre l'opportunità d'essere più
felici.

未来は常により幸福になるための機会を我々に提供して
くれる。

Будущее всегда дает нам возможность стать
более счастливыми.

El futuro siempre nos ofrece la oportunidad de
alegrarnos más.

Life is to be enjoyed.

تمتع بحياتك.

我们该享受生活的乐趣。

La vie est faite pour être vécue pleinement.

Das Leben ist da, um genossen zu werden.

יש להנות מהחיים.

La vita va goduta.

人生とは楽しむべきものである。

Нужно наслаждаться жизнью.

La vida hay que disfrutarla.

Allowing yourself to have fun is a life-long commitment.

السماح لنفسك بالتمتع بالحياة عهد طويل المدى.

享受生活的乐趣是一生的事。

S'autoriser à profiter de la vie est l'engagement de toute une vie.

Es ist eine lebenslange Verpflichtung sich Freude am Leben zu gönnen.

לאפשר לעצמך להנות זו משאת חיים.

Concedere a se stessi di godere è una responsabilità che vincola tutta la vita.

あくせく働くだけが人生ではない。楽しみをもつこもまた
大切な生き甲斐の一つである。

Позволять себе получать удовольствие представляет цель жизни.

El permitirte a ti mismo divertirte es un compromiso que dura toda la vida.

Reach for your highest level of dreams.

عليك الوصول لتحقيق أعلى درجات أحلامك.

追逐自己最大的梦想。

Visez à atteindre le plus haut niveau de vos rêves.

Strebe nach deinen kühnsten Träumen.

נסה להשיג את החלומות המרוחקים ביותר.

Punta ai tuoi sogni più alti.

至上の夢を追い求めなさい。

Достигни своих самых сокровенных мечтаний.

Intenta alcanzar el mayor nivel de tus sueños.

The best is yet to come.

الأفضل في طريقه إلينا.

明天会更好。

Le meilleur est à venir.

Die Zukunft hält das beste noch bereit.

הטוב ביותר עוד לפנינו.

Il meglio deve venire.

焦らずとも道は自然に開けてくるもの。

Лучшее еще впереди.

Lo mejor está por venir.